God See Our Abilities - Not Our Disabilities

GOD'S

Masterpieces

He has a
purpose for
all of us.

I0027162

CORINTHIA PRUITT-STROUD

GOD'S MASTERPIECES
God Sees Our Abilities - Not Our Disabilities

Corinthia Puritt-Stroud
pruittcorinthia@yahoo.com

ISBN 978-1-949826-41-8

Printed in the USA.
All rights reserved

Published by: EAGLES GLOBAL BOOKS | Frisco, Texas
In conjunction with the 2021 Eagles Authors Course
Cover & interior designed by DestinedToPublish.com

Dedication

This book is dedicated to my mother, Barbara Carol Merrideth (1950–2007), who was a wonderful mother. After raising her four biological children, she decided to take on the job of nurturing and caring for children in need. She pursued and secured her foster parenting license in 1992 and began taking in children who needed a home as well as someone to love and care for them.

My mom took on the full capacity of taking care of these children. She set aside time for doctors' appointments, therapy, and other things the kids needed. My mother did not limit herself by finances or anything else to make sure that these kids were stable and had a good foundation. She never allowed the caseworkers to do anything. For the children, she did it all. My mother not only took care of children in need, but she also opened her responsibility up to a greater need: children with disabilities. My mother was a nurse, and her medical career gave her the knowledge and patience to handle what she had chosen. In being a nurse, she had encountered and experienced many things in the hospital, medical facilities, private duty nursing, mental wards, and nursing homes. After a couple of years, my mom stopped foster parenting and started adopting children. In the end, she adopted six children, and all of them had special needs.

Acknowledgments

I acknowledge my husband Anthony Stroud, Sr.; my children Shay, Jasmine, Amarion and Mariah; and my Grand Princess Da'Niyah for your love, patience, and understanding in giving me the time to write this book, because you knew what it meant to me. It took a lot of time from our family life, but you all endured it.

To my sisters Michelle Pruitt and Tammy Pruitt our love for one another stands against anything. You guys have been my rock to go to through it all. I am grateful to have you both as sisters and I love you both dearly!

I would also like to give special acknowledgments to Pastor Lawrence D. Haskin, Sr., and First Lady Minister Sylvia Haskin for their love, spiritual guidance, and support. Their ministry has been part of my stability and success in Christianity as well as in life. I thank you guys for the teaching, because my knowledge of God and his word would not be where it is today if you had not planted that seed, watered, and nurtured it. You both know me as parents would know their child. You both are the givers to what ever is needed and everything you do is out of love. I love you both!

I would also like to thank Lawrence Haskin, Jr., Stefanie Haskin, Nina Goshay, Pastor Walter Adams, Betty Adams, LaVerne Haskin-Scarbrough, Pastor Vincent Anderson, Dr. Minister Karen Anderson, Tiffany Manning, Margaret Wooten, Deacon Christopher Smith, Minister Sheila Smith, Elder Jesse, Minister Darlene, Deacon Leonard Haskin, Coletta Haskin, Johnnie Lenzy Jr., Dena Lenzy and Deacon Eagle Lucia Jones. All your love and support for me and my family has been sincere and from the heart. No matter what I called on all of you to do, you did it with a smile and love. Much gratitude!!!

Contents

Introduction

Some of the world looks at having a disability as one of the worst things that could possibly happen to an individual. They think of being disabled as an untreatable disease. Disabled people are just like everyone else, they just may lack in certain areas. They are special individuals who were created for a purpose like every other human being. God made no mistakes when he created any of us. If we go through the Bible and look back at biblical times, we will see that people were disabled and sick during those times as well. Some people shunned them then, as they do now. No matter what some people try to do, it will never stop God's journey or purpose for his people disabled or not.

God created us in his image and likeness, and no matter what someone is like, God will meet them where they are. We are built like a tree with vines flowing through. On that tree, we are all branches that love, and strengthen one another. From that love and strength comes growth and power. God sees our abilities not our disabilities, because with his grace upon our lives anything is possible. Where, when, how and to whom we are born is all up to him. God knows what we will face before we are even created. We were created for his purpose and to show his miracles. Although some people may be disabled, God has still given them gifts. No matter what the situation is or how you are valued by others, God's gift will still come out through you. The world may see people in different ways, but God does not. He considers all of us his masterpieces.

Disabled people are not all treated the same, and this is part of the reason why some disabled people do not end up in a good place in life. How a disabled person is treated really depends upon the circumstance and the type of disability one has. Some people just do not go to the extent of making sure that disabled people of any kind get the help that they truly need. People with disabilities can be given so many resources and taught how to utilize them, but it does not happen in all cases. In the case of children with disabilities, it must start from the parent. So, if the parent is not advocating for the child or just simply takes what is handed out to them without seeking more throughout the child's life, this leaves the child to be neglected, without the resources that could help them through life. Now this child is growing up with disabilities and will still need help.

Through my personal journey of experience with disabled people, the one thing I have learned is that disabled children and adults are not all the same and do not end up the same when traveling through life. It comes down to how a disabled person really views themselves and whether they are willing to reach out to get the help that they need for themselves and their children. Another major point is whether they have a support system, resources and someone to advocate for them. In the end, it's just like any other person without a disability: self-preservation comes first.

A person must do what needs to be done for themselves or reach out to get the help they need in order to do better and have stability in life. In the end, the biggest struggle for disabled people is having to deal with the world itself. The people in the world who do not view them as normal people. Therefore, some disabled adults and children function most of the time by what other people make their self-worth out to be.

John

My father was an educated man. He not only had a college degree, but he also had several certifications in different trades. When employment became difficult to achieve, he decided to enlist in the army, which was one way of securing some type of finances to take care of his family. After he came home from Vietnam, he was crippled by alcohol and substance abuse. This led him down a bad path. As he spiraled down this path, his mental stability changed. He became abusive to his family I remember when he and my mother could not come to an agreement about us visiting him, he stated that "if he could not see us that day, she would not have us anymore". He then proceeded to pour gasoline in the doorway and set the house on fire. Thank God we survived.

As time went on, he continued to spiral down the wrong path, and due to a bad choice, he became disabled. He was wrestling with someone, and they twisted his neck the wrong way, which paralyzed him on the right side of his body. After that, my father wore a leg brace and walked with a cane permanently. This really changed him to the point of no return. There were many resources for him, but in his mindset, he was unable to be reached. I attribute his disability to developing Post Traumatic Stress Disorder (PTSD) from going to Vietnam. Post-Traumatic Stress Disorder affects a person's mental and emotional stability. This can cause a person to have bad thinking, reactions and decisions, and it can ruin their life. For my father, it caused him to lose control of himself and, in turn, turned his life upside down. He never gave himself a chance at life before dying at 49 years old.

Shay

In the beginning, I never saw any signs of her disability. When she was around the age of six, things started to change with her. Mood swings, depression, emotional instability, anger and hyperactivity became a part of her everyday characteristics. She began to act out in school. I stayed at the school in meetings about her behavior. She was academically enhanced: her grades were superb, and she tested way above her grade. Therefore, the school naturally resisted in giving her an IEP (Individualized Education Program).

After a couple of years of going through in-school and out-of-school suspensions, her third-grade teacher spoke out about what she was experiencing in the classroom with my daughter. It was then that I was contacted by the school psychologist to get the ball rolling. By this time, she was in the fourth grade; it was the end of the school year, and my daughter's behavior had become unbearable. She fought, she was unruly, and this caused the other children to be neglected in their learning. Her teacher, the principal and the psychologist made the decision, with my approval, that she would be allowed to come to school and take her yearly testing, then go home right after.

When she got to fifth grade, she was given an IEP and approved for special education. The department set up the resources that she needed to keep her consistent in class. She also had weekly visits with an outside psychiatrist, which led them to give her the proper testing and evaluations that later showed she had attention deficit hyperactivity disorder. They put her on medication and gave her all the resources she needed to help get her aligned and able to cope. As years went by, she still had episodes, but there were resources put in place to help her.

When my daughter got to high school, it was a different playing field. Instead of giving her supportive resources, they gave her the choice to come to see the psychologist twice a week. I know it was to teach her to be independent as well as to learn self-control, but in a setting of her peers, she did not want to be labeled. Therefore, she started to act out again. I then sat down with the special education department to see what could be done. They said the only thing they could do was call her on the intercom to remind her where to go meet the psychologist, yet it would still be left up to her to go. I found this disturbing, but I had to go along with it.

By this time, my daughter was a sophomore in high school, and she had started getting better at going to see the psychologist on her own. Her grades were superb, and her future looked bright. But then, when the school did her final IEP, the ball broke the window. The team stated to my daughter and me that she would not be able to attend a four-year university and that she would be better off at a city college. When you look at my daughter's school records, she had always been an honor roll student despite she had behavior problems. Therefore, I felt that she was being pushed to the side and labeled.

I then told her to apply for the colleges she wanted to go to and submit them to her dean as she was advised. I do not know if he did this because of what the school had in her records, or if he simply forgot, but the dean never sent her applications out, which meant she had to apply for schools at the last minute. My daughter got accepted at a well-known university and only had to pay out of pocket $4,000 a year. Only God could have made that possible. She did well in the beginning, but halfway through, she lost control of being on task. I believe this was due to her high school not preparing the paperwork for the right resources to help her at college, but the great thing was that she had mentors who helped her along the way.

After completing her four years, she still had credits to earn, so she decided to come home and finish. My daughter enrolled at a university here and immediately made the dean's list. When people say no, God says yes.

Today my daughter has a great job with excellent pay and benefits. Her disability was unknown for years. Only God knew what she would endure, therefore he ordered a path for her – she just had to get on it. She still has episodes, but she knows how to handle them without medication, but through prayer.

Amarion

My son was not born disabled, but through an accident of him falling and hitting his head on a hard surface, he ended up with traumatic brain injury. He was diagnosed with hydrocephalus, which is water on the brain. During the first year of his life, the neurologist had a difficult time placing the shunt in his head and tubing in his body. Every couple of months, they had to cut into his head in order to drain the fluids out, because was the only way that he could live. The horrible side effect of this is the scarring on his head. He also had uneven bones in his legs, seizures and other minor complications.

When the neurosurgeon finally got the shunt and tubing in place, they did not function properly. I was then told that there was the possibility he would have to wear a helmet, leg braces and be bedridden the rest of his life, because his head would be so large that it could cause him to be unable to walk. God said no, and my son beat all the odds. His final surgery was a success. The shunt and tubing began to pump out the excess fluids, and after a few years, he was no longer having seizures.

My son got a great start with his education. At nine months old, he entered early intervention in a public school and was given every resource he needed and then some. He stayed in the same classroom with the same teachers for five years. His academics were impeccable. My son learned to read and write before he was five years old. He was in special education, but he rose above that level. He has always been on the honor roll. During his IEP, they were not able to set limits on him. The team just put resources and tools in place to support him where he needed it. My son leaves for college soon and has a full academic scholarship. He obtained employment on his own at a well-known restaurant as a cook, and he is doing extremely well for his first job. He has been there over a year and has been offered a promotion. He takes pride in his job, and his work ethics are impeccable. He did not let anyone, or anything stop him from achieving his goals.

Jasmine

My adopted daughter was born disabled, and she developed more disabilities due to negligence and proper care while in the womb. She was born with extra chromosomes, which has caused her to have Turner's Syndrome and many other illnesses in her endocrine system. She was diagnosed as having vision and speech impairment, as well as being cognitively delayed. Jasmine also shows some signs of mental illness and physical disablement. She was never treated for many of her illnesses until she was about 11 years old, because most of them were not found at an early age. As a result of this, her disabilities were unable to be addressed properly.

My daughter was never given early intervention, because no one felt the need to address her disabilities. She was put into special education around second grade only because they found out she could not read. During the process, she never learned how to read or do math. She passed grade to grade simply because of being in special education. When she got to high school, they said that if she made it to college, it would have to be a community college. They also said she would only be able to accomplish a two-year degree. The school had already set limitations on her education, which seemed as if she would only receive the minimum services. I did not agree with them at all, but this is the recommendation that they gave her.

After high school, she was enrolled in a co-op program which was supposed to prepare her for life and school. I trusted in trying this method first because I was assured that it would help her, but the only thing they did was use her to work for slave wages and go on field trips. My daughter was a young adult, not a child. I took her out of the program and enrolled her in an online university, with me sitting in as her tutor. She did extremely well until she lost complete focus in school and could not complete her second year of college.

As an adult , Jasmine is having a hard time coping with life and staying on track. She does not want to deal with her disabilities at all. My daughter refuses treatment and does not like to talk about it. There was one instance where she had to be placed in a facility to get help, but it was useless. They kept her for a week, put her on in-house medication while she was there, and sent her home. In my mind, I pondered how this was helping her – and it did not. Once she came home, she was okay for a little while, but then her issues started to come back again. The diagnosis was anxiety. To my knowledge, anxiety makes one feel worried and uneasy, not defensive and angry. Whatever her mental illness is, it makes her hard to deal with on many levels. It is hard to have a simple conversation with her about her disabilities, especially when it is time to see a doctor. Therefore, I have decided to make her appointments and sit in on her doctor's appointments. She is now getting the proper evaluations, and progress is being made.

My daughter has had many jobs through temp agencies. She goes to work when she is supposed to and is never late. Jasmine does a great job when she is shown what to do. Yet on the other hand sometimes she does not understand things well and her physical disabilities get in the way of her doing her job effectively. In the end she does her best to stay on task, because she wants to be productive and financially stable.

Corinthia

I was not born disabled. In 2009, I became disabled because of a medication allergy. Cephalosporin is in the penicillin family, which I am allergic to, but I was not aware of that medication allergy at the time when they gave it to me. It put me in a coma for three weeks, and I acquired meningitis and encephalitis. I was healed from both, but during the process, the full use of my legs did not come back when I awoke. Therefore, I have limitations on my mobility.

I needed help doing everything in the beginning, which made me lazy and dependent upon others. What I found out during this period of my life was that I had given up spiritually and mentally, and this is what made my physical being disappear. It has been extremely hard for me physically. Hearing about my experience, people would probably wonder how or why my disability is mental. It is mental because that is where my disability dwells. I am here to tell you that when your mind is off, the body follows that direction.

Along the way to recovery, I had another accident that required me to have surgery on my left leg. I walked around for six months to a year with a hole the size of a small grapefruit opening in my leg. It was horrible at first, but somehow this accident made me stronger. I was able to finish my bachelor's degree while recovering and still attend church. God saw me through it all, and he set everything in place for my mental, emotional and physical healing.

It took me from 2009 until 2017 to decide I wanted to live. I began to do more for myself and take control of my life. I concluded that disability had no place in my life. I walk with a limp and things take time for me, but it is okay. I have learned to do what I can and not what the world has expected of me. It took me a long time to get in the right headspace of what I should be doing and not what I am overextending myself to do.

– Chapter 1 –

The Arrival

When people decide to bring a life into the world, they have no idea that the child could be disabled. Being disabled or having a disabled child(ren) is not the end of the world for anyone; it's just a different type of path that one must walk through in order to have a fruitful and stabile life.

A family's DNA is the one thing we cannot avoid when it comes to any type of illness or disability, because it is in the chemical (DNA) make-up of our bodies. When a child inherits a disability, some of the time there is a family medical history that has already been made known to the doctors. Therefore, that will help the doctors understand how to move forward in treating the child during pregnancy, in childbirth and after they are born. The downside is when the mother of the child does not know any family medical history and must ponder where it came from; in these cases, it can take the doctor many years to get the right diagnosis and treat it. This happens a lot, and shocking as it is, some mothers don't take it seriously or even take it into consideration before bearing children. It is important for mothers to know the medical history of their family as well as that of the child's father's family. It is also important to know that not only are disabilities inherited, but they can also come about through negligence while pregnant, accidents, and birth defects.

Inherited Disorders

Most inherited disabilities usually center around mental illnesses, which are disorders that affect the mind and the ability to function on a day-to-day basis. Mental disorders can sometimes be hard to distinguish one from another, because each person is different. Therefore, it is best to know the family's medical history, because it will give the medical team clarity on where to start running evaluations for treatment.

Some prominent mental illness disorders are inheritable. Most of these are tied to one another.

- Psychotic disorders: a group of serious illnesses that affect the mind (such as schizophrenia)

- Personality disorders: "any of various psychological disorders that are characterized by persistent inflexible or impaired patterns of thought and behavior that usually cause difficulties in forming and maintaining interpersonal relationships and in meeting the daily demands of one's personal and work life and that typically become apparent during adolescence or early adulthood" (Merriam-Webster)

- Depression: feelings of severe despondency and dejection

- Bipolar: a mental condition marked by the alternation of depression and elation

- Panic/anxiety disorders: disorders that revolve around fear or worry about a certain outcome of something

Birth Defects

Birth defects can range from something as simple as not getting fluid and drainage completely out of the ears, nose, eyes or throat to something extreme like allowing the infant to lose too much oxygen, which can impose many medical and mental disorders. When a disability comes from a birth defect, it is usually something parents or families are not prepared for, and most of the time, it is unknown until the infant begins to show signs of an issue. When this happens, the parents then began to try and find out what the problem is by having many tests done. When they find out, then they try to figure where it came from, especially if it is not in the parents' medical files. Once they know where the problem came from, parents want to make sure that their child is okay and able to get the treatment that they may need in order to survive through life.

Accidental Disabilities

An accidental disability can come from something like wrong medication or a physical accident (car accident, being shot or stabbed, etc.). This type of disability can be life changing, because it can mess with a person's mental and emotional capacity as well. When people go from living their lives one way to having to adjust to a physical change in their day-to-day living, it can be a difficult task for some.

Negligence

Negligence is the worst kind of disability that an individual can acquire, simply because it can be prevented. When I speak of negligence, I am referring to a mother being pregnant and doing things that are not healthy for herself, which are also harmful for the child she is carrying. Most alcoholics and drug addicts are not aware of how much damage can be done to a fetus. When a fetus receives an overload of alcohol and drugs through the blood system, there is a wide range of mental, emotional and physical disabilities that the unborn fetus can acquire while still in the womb.

This type of disability is not to be taken lightly, because it is almost as simple as saying that the mother is already a negligent and abusive parent by not taking into consideration that she has another life growing inside of her. Once this child is born, they must live with what they have acquired due to the parent's negligence. If the government does not step in and take the child, the child will continue to go through negligence and abuse, because the mother still may not get any help with her addictions. Either way, these infants go through a lifelong ordeal. Some people do not understand how horrific this can be for a child in this situation. If you really investigate the life of an alcoholic or addict, then you can come to an understanding of why the child act/reacts in the way they do.

– Chapter 2 –

External View

Labeling

Disabled individuals are conveniently labeled for some reason. I believe people do this out of ignorance, lack of knowledge and fear. The ignorant ones are just plain heartless and have no compassion for others. They do not understand things, and they do not want to understand. They have their own opinion, and for some reason, they value what they believe and try to get others to see things from their point of view. They will even go as far as finding statistics and other information to back them up somewhat.

Lack of knowledge is one of the worst reasons why some people make judgments in all the wrong ways. When people lack knowledge about people with a disability, they tend to put their own label on them. Some people speak untruth, make up experiences and even build up walls of fear. Fear will take one to a whole different dimension. Some people have a fear of certain disabilities, especially the mentally impaired. They call them crazy, retarded and many other names. Disabled people are not all physically disabled, and they are not all mentally ill. It is the labeling of some people that brings in the confusion about disabled people. Some people do not realize that mentally ill individuals have no idea of how they are acting; they are merely caught up in their own mindset.

Containment

Disabled individuals are categorized into their own group. It does not matter what the disability is or how it came about, these individuals are put in containment by certain people. They are looked at like a disease, preyed upon, singled out and shunned by some of society. Although some of their disabilities are not due to their own acts or negligence, all disabled individuals are treated as they do not exist.

They live in this world yet are invisible to society. Disabled individuals move through life like a ghost or spirit unseen. They build their own world around them to the point that it makes them feel comfortable with a small quality of life. There is nothing wrong with being comfortable with the life you have, but why should they feel that they are not one of the "norms"? They try to fit in, but some of society will not allow them. It seems like some people can just pick up on how people look, speak and behave, and assume that they are disabled. So, they make them feel very uncomfortable or belittled to the point where disabled people will not go beyond certain barriers in living among society.

It has gotten so bad that I have seen children not interacting with other children because of the adults. Most children do not know about other children having disabilities, but some adults say things about others that children should not hear. Therefore, the children get the idea that disabled children do not belong among the "normal" children. Most children follow what they are taught until they are old enough to know right from wrong, but sometimes what they are taught will grow with them, and they will grow up making fun of disabled individuals. Until this stops, generations of children growing into adults will continue to have this outlook on people with disabilities.

Injustice

Disabled individuals have been served injustice for many years, and it is senseless. No one seems to respect them for any reason at all. If you look around in the world today, many disabled people have been attacked not just by other people but sometimes by law enforcement as well. They disregard disabled people or treat them with no respect. I understand that law enforcement has protocol to follow to do what is safe for them and the public, yet if you see that a person is somewhat mentally or physically unstable, you should have a little compassion for them. Law enforcement should find other ways to handle those situations. Even when they take someone to jail and lock them up in the beginning, they are not trying to hear that the person is disabled. It takes the disabled person's attorney to bring it up and enforce it to the court that their client needs to have a mental evaluation.

The downside to this is that sometimes lawyers use this tactic to get their clients off, which in turn makes it bad for people who are truly disabled and need more resources other than being locked in jail among criminals who can really harm them. It is also possible that mentally disabled people can be driven to the point of harming other prisoners, which is not a good thing for the disabled individual, because they can end up in a psychiatric hospital for the duration of their imprisonment. How does that help them with their disability? It doesn't, because in some cases disabled people are just being institutionalized and given medication that controls them as their treatment. They may get therapy, but no other life resources. When they are ready for release, they still sometimes must be at a certain level, just like parole, to get out. Sometimes they do not get out, and when they do, it is upon certain conditions that may or may not give room for them to do well. Again, how does this enhance their quality of life?

– Chapter 3 –

Internal View

Self-Worth

Self-worth is the key to how fruitful your life can be. What people do not understand is, if they do not hold value in their own lives, who will? Some of the world sees you as you see yourself, and others view you from their own perspectives. What some people think of you is one thing, but how you see yourself is what is most important. Disabled people tend to value their self-worth by how the world values them. They have somehow lost the drive and ambition to do life.

Looking through the eyes of the disabled can be a scary view, because to them, all hope is lost. Can you imagine being in the world where it seems as though you're present, but you're not? This is truly how a disabled person feels. It does not matter whether it's a mental, physical or emotional disability; this is how disabled people feel. They cannot seem to adjust in society no matter how hard they try. Some of society tells them they do not belong in the world with "normal" people. Therefore, disabled individuals put themselves in a box.

Disabled people get comfortable living inside a four-wall perimeter. Within this perimeter, they do what they know how to do, never expanding to do more than that. They will not go beyond what will put them in a position to deal with society up close and personal. They will accept the handouts that the world throws at them. They do not know how to function beyond a certain point and they will stray away from others.

Disabled people do not know how to blend in with society; they just adjust to the rules of the world. These rules tell them that they are dumb, retarded, and not on the level to live among "normal" people. This will cause something to happen inside of them, which is a defense mechanism against people in general. I have seen these many times with one of my children who is cognitively delayed. Through her whole life, she has felt defensive toward everything you say to her that does not line up with what she understands. With disabled people, we must understand that their thought process and physical being are never going to be the same as ours; it is going to be what settles within them. So, you must ask yourself, what is normal? You do not have to be disabled to be different from the world. I think it is just a lack of knowledge of things.

Confusion

Disabled individuals live in a world of confusion. This is because of the way some of society has made them view themselves. Although disabled people may not understand a lot, they can feel through emotions that they are being targeted. Therefore, it makes them confused about their own lives . This may sound a little backwards, but it is true. I speak from experience with my own disabled daughter. If the way she is treated makes her feel good about herself and she can somewhat see where she's at in life, she feels confident. The moment she is made to feel anything different about herself, such as negativity or a lack of clarity about things, she becomes confused about herself and her life.

When some disabled individuals have so much mentally coming towards them at one time and cannot filter it, they lose understanding, and it begins to work on the heart. Some disabled people do not have control over their mind or their emotions without the proper help and resources.

Emotional Instability

Emotions run wild when it comes to mental and sometimes physical disabilities. The mind, body and heart work separately yet together. What a person feels, does and thinks are all different, but if they somehow blend, it can be a deadly combination, especially for a disabled person. If that thought process is messed up, it can mess with their heart and stagnate their physical being. Some disabled people tend to hurt more from the heart than from the mind.

This simply goes back to the main ingredient which is the thought process. I think the reason for this because they just want to fit in and feel like they are someone. Some people in the world have a way of inflicting pain to the heart by shooting daggers where it really hurts. It is enough that a disabled person's mind has a hard time adjusting, yet they must try and keep up with what some of society is doing to them or expecting them to do.

Differences

Disabled individuals are singled out in many ways especially from other children. Children can be cruel to their disabled peers. For example, in school, they are put in a separate classroom or on a short school bus. These two small things that have caused some children to treat them differently. Yes, they do need to be in an environment that is protective as well as stable for them, but I believe that they can function in a regular classroom setting or on a regular school bus with is an assistant to monitor them.

Disabled children look at all children the same and only wants to make new friends, not understanding why the other children will not interact with them. I have personally followed the trend of watching how "normal" children react to disabled children. Children see the world differently through their eyes, but when certain things catch their attention, they began to exert their curiosity. They want to know what is what.

Explaining what is going on with a disabled child to another child is not easy, but it also depends on who does the explaining. A person who is ignorant, fearful or not knowledgeable about disabled children is the wrong person to explain this to anyone, especially a child. If a child sees others making fun of, staying away from or saying bad things about a disabled child or adult, they will take the wrong actions toward them until they are confronted and straightened out. What children must understand is that a disability is not a bad thing. It simply means a person has different qualities within themselves.

– Chapter 4 –

Medical Treatment

You would assume that in the United States of America, everyone would get equal and good medical treatment, but that is not the case. There is limited care given to those who do not seek further treatment, do not have money or quality medical insurance. If you take a child to the doctor, stating that you have concerns about the child(ren) having any type of mental or medical issue, sometimes the doctor tells you they're not old enough. I have been told this numerous of times.

This stagnates the progress of the disabled or sickly child(ren) in getting the proper help that is needed. This can cause a parent to go through many mental and emotional adjustments when it comes to finding ways of helping their children and getting the resources, they need to stabilize their disabilities or illnesses. By the time the child gets to a certain age, the disability or illness has gotten worse. The doctor then begins to ask you why you didn't bring them in before now. By now, the parent is looking dumbfounded because they have been told over the years by doctors that they cannot treat the child(ren) until they get over a certain age.

What the world fails to realize is that a lot of parents' hands are tied due to the lack of information, finances, and good medical insurance. Sometimes parents just don't know what to do or do not have certain information or criteria that others have in order to successfully find the right doctors for treatment. I have experienced the good and bad ends of medical treatment with two of my children. My son has been getting excellent medical care from the time he had traumatic brain injury up until today. He has seen the best specialists, surgeons and doctors all his life. In fact, his treatment was so good that he doesn't have to see his neurologist anymore.

On the other hand, my daughter was not given the proper treatment or seen by the right doctors for any of her illnesses or disabilities during her earlier years of life. By the time I took her to the doctor and it was addressed, I was told that there was nothing they could really do at this point. She's really at a point in her life where she has truly ignored every issue that she's dealing with, because even as an adult, she is still not seeing doctors who would give her the proper care that she needs. I must make sure that she is on top of her medical needs. I must constantly stay on her about taking yearly tests, making sure that she has all her medications and taking them.

I must constantly ask her how she's feeling or if anything unusual is going on with her, because she won't say anything. This is not a good thing at all, because with as many underlying issues as she has, they can really shut her body down, and she could die. It is not that she does not care about her health or life; it is because she is mentally incapable of making the right decisions for herself. In her mindset, if she's able to cope with day-to-day life, she's okay. Disabled people or those overseeing their medical needs must seek out the right doctors, because they need to be treated, not just labeled. Some disabled people may not have money, proper medical insurance or information about proper medical treatment, but those resources are available if they seek them.

– Chapter 5 –

Parenting with Disabilities

Becoming a parent is a great joy for many people. The flip side is that as a first-time parent, you don't know what to expect or what to do. Parents get a lot of advice from other people, use self-help books, watch documentaries or simply follow their own parent's upbringing. All these resources are okay, because the parents will either correct the mistakes that cause issues in their child(ren's) lives or come to a stable ground where they have learned better parenting skills.

Although one might not think at first that people with disabilities would have children, it does happen, which can be quite the challenge. Parenting with disabilities can be a lot harder, depending on the disability. Sometimes disabled parents stretch themselves in order to achieve just the basic skills. A parent's mental and emotional disabilities can reduce the quality of parenting that a child(ren) can get from that person. First of all a mentally disabled person is lacking full understanding and knowledge of certain aspects of life. Therefore, they are already missing vital mental capabilities, which will prohibit them from achieving certain parenting skills.

Some physically disabled parents have the mental capacity to raise a child(ren), but they cannot do certain physical parental duties or activities for and with the child. When this happens, it can really affect a child(ren) both mentally and physically. The child(ren) can be emotionally withdrawn as well as depressed, because they are not taking part in physical activities on a regular basis that a child(ren) would normally do. It also can mess with their dietary health Some parent's disabilities can enable them from cooking and providing healthy meals. The child(ren) can form unhealthy eating habits that can cause medical issues such as high blood pressure, diabetes, and high cholesterol. In the end, theses illnesses can lead to more illnesses.

Don't mistake me for saying that a parent with disabilities cannot raise a child. It just requires them to have that extra patience, as well as a stable and strong support system, and the proper resources set in place to help them do what needs to be done for themselves and for the child(ren).

I can relate to this because I do have a physical disability. Although I have a lot of help in my house, I still try to make sure that my children are in a stable and functioning environment when it comes to their health, physical, and mental wellbeing . I do sit down a lot when I cook, but I cook every day to make sure that my children are getting a healthy meal. On the other hand, physically, there is not a lot that I can do for long periods of time. It messes with me mentally because I am not physically able to do a lot of things that I used to do with my children. It drains me emotionally just thinking about it. It also puts me in a setting where I feel depressed, which makes me feel fatigued and tired a lot.

This fatigue and tiredness cause me to say no to my children a lot about physically doing things with them or going places. My youngest child confessed to me how she felt about my disability. She felt that I was taking her life away because her life is limited, because of my disability. People may think that kids can adjust and adapt to anything, but that is not true. It makes them feel alone and rejected. This can cause children to find other outlets to comfort them in good and bad ways.

Mind Over Matter

When a parent and their child(ren) both have disabilities, it brings two difficult situations together that are more than likely to blow up badly at some point, which can cause a great deal of suffering for both the child(ren) and the parent. Children already have a hard time coping with being mentally, emotionally or physically disabled. They're already dealing with the world and the way that they are viewed, as well as the quality of life they are experiencing. Now add in a parent who is not getting the medical treatment or resources they need to be stable for themselves, which would also enable them to see and help with their child(ren's) disability.

Some parents have been dealing with mental disabilities all their lives and have never had the proper treatment, resources or support from anyone. This can become even more toxic, because now the child(ren) is left on their own to try and figure things out on their own until they can get some type of help or resources.

Even if the child can get help outside of the home, it still is bad for the child, because the parent will not be able to cope or help with the child's disability due to their own setbacks from their own disability.

Therefore, it is extremely necessary that when an adult has a disability, whether male or female, it is addressed as soon as possible, because there is always the possibility that a disabled person, just like a person who is not disabled, can bear children. The bottom line is that both parent and child(ren) must have the proper treatment in order to achieve stability in their lives, because if not, it can have a tragic outcome. An overwhelmed parent can be toxic. Their caring and nurturing can become abusive and neglectful towards the child. This is what I call the dark side for the child.

The dark side is when a child(ren) is going through trauma and abuse by a disabled parent(s). No one will ever know unless the child tells, or they witness what is going on. Most of the time the child(ren) may think what they are going through is normal, because it is a normal way of living for them. Also, child(ren) love their parents and will not tell because they want to be with them. This can end tragically for the child(ren). If no one knows or help the child(ren) they could end up in a bad place emotionally, mentally or possibly dead.

Stabilizing

Being a parent with disabilities trying to raise a child(ren) with disabilities may seem like a difficult way to live, but it is not. There are many things that can be done to stabilize the lifestyle of both parent and child(ren). First, the parent must have the support and resources that they need for their own disabilities. The disabled parent must have a structured life in order to even begin to raise their child(ren), disabled or not. The disabled parent must have consistency every day in their life in order to understand what they need to do, just for themselves to be stable. Once the parent has all their resources in place, they can then understand what they must do for their child(ren) who is disabled.

Sometimes it could be a little difficult, depending on the disabilities that the parent and the child(ren) have, but there are many resources that can help both parents and child cope with one another's disabilities. In the end both parent and child(ren) lives will begin to balance out and then everyone will be on the same playing field.

– Chapter 6 –

Education

The education of disabled individuals can be good, bad or unfair. If a disability is found in the earlier stages of a person's life, their education can start through early intervention and be followed up later with IEPs.

As a child grows older, the educational needs widen; therefore, it is always good to keep the child in some type of educational training throughout their life, even as an adult, because as they grow older, their mindset will change even with the disability. Without continual training, they will sink backwards, because they are not in an environment where they are on a consistent educational plan.

Early Educational Intervention

Early educational intervention is the best thing you can give a child with any type of disability. Early intervention addresses the needs of the disability as well as the growth path in a child's life, and it is also crucial to their ability to adapt to the knowledge of things. Early intervention can be in the home or a school setting.

There are some schools that will take children as young as six months old and begin to work with them on their disabilities and keep them on the path with their education, life skills, potty training and so forth. The teachers will also assess the child for other resources they may need as they grow older and make the connections for those resources. It literally gives the child a fighting chance at a proper education. These educational resources allow the child to be able to function at their level and not be discouraged. It moves them right along at their pace, and sometimes children excel beyond that pace.

Early intervention starts by following the children throughout their educational years. You do not have to keep going back and forth to the school begging for resources. Early intervention opens the door for a child to have an IEP. Although they are growing older into an adolescent stage, they still are going to need that extra support to push them through. Therefore, it is essential that their support system and resources stay with them throughout their entire educational life. Even when they attempt to go to college, those files should go with them, because it will let the college professors know how to work with the disabled student.

Educational/Skills Training

Educational and skills training is also needed for disabled people. It is an outlet for them to learn more. This educational training does not necessarily have to be geared toward college; it can be life tools or areas that are greatly needed for that individual person. Disabled people can learn about health, finances, travel, religion, parenting skills and other assets. This type of training can help find out what a person with disabilities is capable of and good at. In the end, it will be skills and education that can stabilize them in being fruitful in their lives. It will also give them the self-assurance and confidence to stand on their own, take some risks and giant steps toward things they would not do before but feel strong enough to do now.

Parental Educational Support

For a disabled child to be successful in school, parents should start addressing their educational needs when the child is very young, because some disabilities can cause them to be behind their peers. If those educational resources are not there at an early age, it can do damage to their academics and learning process. Parents also must push for their disabled children to strive higher than where they are or what they are learning, because they should want their child to stay at their grade level throughout their educational years. The reality is, as a parent, you do not want your twelfth grader graduating high school at an eighth-grade academic level.

Parents must be very supportive all the way through their child's education. That support should include making sure that their child is in the right educational programs from an early age. A parent should also pay attention and be involved in everything that their child is doing from the time that they start in early intervention all the way up to college. A parent needs to know exactly what resources their child is getting and how the child is adapting to those resources. A parent also must push for their children to get better resources if the resources they are getting are not working for them. The main ingredient to all of this is a parent knowing the rights that the child and parents have when it comes to education.

– Chapter 7 –

Employment

Gainful employment can be easy or hard, depending on the disabled individual. The reason why it can be hard is that disabled people sometimes do not have the physical or mental capability to perform certain tasks. Therefore, gaining employment in certain industries is very hard for them. Employers have goals that must be met on the job. Some disabled individuals may have mental and physical limitations on what they can do. This already opens the door to say you're not capable of obtaining employment.

I have seen some disabled people try to do jobs that they are physically or mentally incapable of doing, but they try their best to do it. They really don't want to be labeled as a disabled employee, so they will try their best to fit in until it runs out for them. A lot of jobs say they do not discriminate, yet they make excuses for why they can no longer employ the disabled. On the other hand, some employers will work with the disabled because they must have a certain quota of disabled people working for them through government programs. The bottom line is that disabled people have a right to employment in their capacity.

Job Training

Having someone to stand over you all day at your job speaking derogatory things to you as if you are dumb, is a horrible experience. Disabled individuals will do well if they enter a job training program that is designed to train them and give them the knowledge about the job they will do. Job training programs for the disabled can give them a sense of direction, confidence and independence when it comes to them seeking employment. Job training programs for the disabled can help them get into jobs that they never thought they would ever work before. For a disabled person, this is a sure way to learn a trade and get a decent-paying job.

I know this is true because I've seen it firsthand with my daughter. I've seen how the jobs treat her when they figure out that she is disabled, and that is why I told her she needs to enroll in a job training program for the disabled. That way, she can obtain employment and keep it, because she will be trained for it and will be able to stay on task.

– Chapter 8 –

Journey to Connection

In order to truly help a disabled person, we must have a connection with them in a greater capacity. There are many things that can begin that journey into connecting with a person with disabilities. We must remember that they already feel lost and abandoned, as if they do not belong or do not matter to society. Therefore, we must show them the opposite of what they've been feeling or experiencing throughout their lives. It feels horrible to be brushed off and feel worthless, like people will just talk to you and tell you anything because of a disability.

There are a lot of people today who do not really look at me as being physically disabled because they don't see everything about me, but only what they see when they're in my presence. Therefore, it is hard to make that connection with anyone to make that journey. This connection is not a pity party. It is not about asking people to feel sorry for disabled people. It's just about asking people to see those with disabilities for who they are, recognize they need help, and what they can do to help them. If some people will do this, it can work. It can build relationships and trust. It will take time to get disabled people to open up and trust you, but by the grace of God, it can be done.

Love

Love conquers all. Showing people that you love no matter what their situation is can work miracles. If we all functioned in love, we would accomplish a lot of things, especially when it comes to helping others and always doing the right thing – or at least most of the time. Love is all some people simply want. Even if a disabled person is not able to understand clearly or do things at a higher physical capacity, just showing them the love and compassion, you have for them and for helping them would make them try to do more for themselves. God loves us despite everything, and his love can come through us to share with others.

"For God so loved the world, that he gave his only Son, that whoever believes in him should not perish but have eternal life." (John 3:16, ESV)

"Let all that you do be done in love." (1 Corinthians 16:14, ESV)

"And over all these virtues put on love, which binds them all together in perfect unity." (Colossians 3:14, NIV)

Understanding

Having knowledge and understanding things is the root to getting things accomplished. When there is no knowledge or understanding about mentally, emotionally and physically disabled people, how can you accomplish the work of helping them? When you're dealing with the mentally disabled, you must put yourself in their mindset to understand how they think. We must remember that being mentally disabled means that they are not receiving things mentally in the same way as a person without a mental disability. Therefore, it is essential that we pay attention and cover all avenues of trying to understand where they are mentally at the moment, we begin to connect with them. If we do not, it will make our job harder, because their thought process is different from ours. With disabled people, there are two major understandings that people must have in order to help them on their journey: their disability and their need.

1. Disability

Knowing someone's disability is where you will start, because then you will be able to extend yourself and provide resources to help them. Without knowing the type of disability someone has, how can one help them? Therefore, it is essential for the world to take the time to understand different disabilities that people have. No individual disability acts totally the same as another, but there are always common factors that ring out, which will give you some knowledge as to where to begin your journey with that individual. Some mentally or physically disabled people can function in greater capacity than others. This does not mean that they don't need any help. It just means that the resources you must give them would be different. The fact is, it does not matter whether one disability is worse than the next; the moral thing to do is to give everyone the help and resources that they need.

2. The Needs

Once you've learned about someone's disability, then you also must come to understand their needs, because this is very important in helping disabled people on their journey to a healthier and more fruitful life. Their needs go beyond just someone spending time with them or doing things for them, and every disability has a different set of needs. We can look at a physical disability and say basically what the need might be, yet when we go in deeper, the person might need more than that, or possibly less. You must also be careful with physical disabilities, because they can turn into mental and emotional disabilities that are undetected.

Have you ever wondered why this person is not getting better physically when they're getting a treatment? It can be an underlying issue of a mental or emotional disability (possibly depression) due to their physical disability. When it comes to mental and emotional needs, the stakes are even higher and it takes years of resources and commitment to bring them mentally and emotionally where they should be. The reason I say this is because some mental and emotional disabilities can cause people to go into other elements such as depression and PTSD. This can string a person along for life because it takes so much out of them mentally and emotionally, often to the point that they must have medication to control it because they cannot do it on their own. Not all disabilities require the same resources, so the bottom line is making sure that mental, emotional and physical disabilities are assessed to the fullest to make sure that the needs of everyone with a disability is met.

Building Bridges

In order to start and complete the journey of connection with individuals who are disabled, we must build bridges. What I mean by building bridges is taking tiny steps one at a time that will connect each phase to the next to make it make sense for them. Once it makes sense for them, then it's easier for them to elevate to a higher level from the disability capacity that they are in. For example, take a person who is mentally disabled and is not able to understand   something as simple as traveling on the bus. Well, you must start out with what you're trying to get them to do. Once they comprehend that, then you can begin adding on more, and so forth. It may seem as if you are treating them like a child or taking baby steps, but you must understand that a mentally disabled person is not holding information the way we do, which may mean they're not able to hold multitudes of information at one time, so you have to build a bridge to help them understand what is going on.

The physically disabled may be a little bit different when it comes to the process of building bridges, because they can physically feel the reaction from what is being done with them. Physical therapy can overload because a person has so much muscle movement in the 30 minutes to an hour, depending on the need. The physically disabled must adjust slowly before moving into the next stage in order to build up not only physically but mentally as well.

Connecting with an emotionally disabled person can be a extremely difficult task when trying to start that journey of connection and build bridges, because their disability sits between physical and mental disabilities. One can only be emotionally disabled, but sometimes when a person is mentally and physically disabled, it messes with their emotions. Emotional disorders also affect the heart and mind in the way one thinks. So, therefore, you must be very careful when you're trying to connect with such a person, as they could become aggressive and violent. The steps to building bridges with this type of disorder must be carefully planned and placed in even smaller steps, because you do not want to trigger anything that may blow up on the spur of the moment. You must start with getting that person to trust you and also make what you are doing make sense to them.

I do believe that building bridges is a better way to help with the journey of connection because it is a way to understand a person piece by piece rather than experiencing the whole being of a person at one time. When we experience people piece by piece, we get to know and understand them better. When we get the whole being of a person at one time, especially in certain situations, we really have no idea what we are getting. We can be getting someone who only has a certain disability, but because they are so overwhelmed within themselves and what is going on around them, you begin to see a whole lot of other different things that may not be disabilities but rather attributes of the disabilities they have.

Removing Weights

When a person is disabled, they have a lot of pressure on them. You must remember that they are labeled from day one. At least ten pounds of pressure are dropped on them every day of their life. These weights can come from rejection, not feeling loved, not having a support system, feeling worthless and many other things. As these weights begin to weigh heavy on them throughout their lives, it can become overwhelming to them and put them in a position where they just feel like a mountain is on them. So, one of the major things to do when you begin your journey to help a disabled person is to help them take off the layers of weights that have been dropped on them their entire life.

I know from experience that when I became physically disabled, it was a lot for me to handle, and even watching the world from my point of view was horrible to me, because it was then that I learned that people do not respect or care about people with disabilities. I carried so much weight, and it took me from 2009 to 2017 to realize I had to remove those weights for me to have a more fruitful and enjoyable life. Can you imagine someone who has dealt with this all their life?

Introducing

Introducing is a major factor in helping disabled people on their journey to a more successful and fruitful life. A person who is taking the journey with them must introduce them to the new them. When doing this, they must set up a timeline showing the disabled person where they are now and where they can be when they have reached that goal. This timeline journey will also show them where they are making progress in their life. The first thing disabled people must understand is their disability and how it affects them.

Once they have learned this and come to an understanding of it, it will be easy to introduce their new self to them. I use the term "new self" because on this journey, they will find out more things about themselves that they can see and accept in the right way, outside of what was told to them from day one. What God created them to be will now be visible to them and to the world.

Encouraging

Encouragement is a very powerful word. Everyone needs encouragement, no matter what they're trying to achieve. With disabled people, they need someone to give them that pep talk to push them ahead and make them feel as if they are accomplishing something, even if it is a small task. A lot of people need this, yet disabled people need it even more, because some of the world has already told them that they are nothing. To simply say "Job well done, I'm proud of you, you can do more" says a lot to someone, rather than saying "You're dumb, you don't do anything right" or "You're not worth spending time with." Making them feel appreciated simply for who they are is a form of encouragement.

No, we don't want them to think that they're special just because they have a disability, but we want them to feel that they are a person too, that they have a voice and that they should be heard and not just seen. They may not be able to do what the "normal" people can do, but disabled people have a capacity to do things that others cannot do. We're on the journey to connect with them, encourage them and help them learn to appreciate themselves. We must think in terms of focusing not on what they cannot do, but on what they are able to do.

Commitment

Commitment speaks volumes in any individual. When you are helping someone or doing anything, your commitment must be there. You cannot get tired or weary, and you cannot just simply give up because you don't feel like you are connecting or reaching that goal. Disabled people must see that you are committed to them for them to commit themselves to doing better things in life. I know my family was 120% in when I came out of my coma. They helped me do everything, they encourage me to try to do more, but the thing I really love them for is that they never made me feel worthless. They always kept me at a point where I knew I was loved, and everything they were helping me with and doing for me was for me to get better.

Victory

The building bridges method is a victory. It is a great method to start with because it goes in steps and phases, and one will be able to see the progress that is being made. If one continues to use the building bridges method over and over and over, everyone will really begin to see things open up as disabled people develop more self-assurance. They will see they do matter and are important. They will strive to do more for themselves. Disabled people will then begin to advocate for themselves and their disabled child(ren). Relationships will be built with all involved, which will bring enlightenment and an understanding of why this is needed for all parties. In the end, God will get the glory.

– Chapter 9 –

Advocating

In order to help disabled people, we must be advocates for them. In advocating for them, we must think of their needs and what is best for them, not our own needs or the world's needs. We cannot just simply put them in a box, do the bare minimum and say this is all they need. We must assess the needs related to the disability and figure out everything the person needs, and once we do that, we can then begin to advocate to the government, the doctors and the treatment centers.

The world goes by statistics and protocol, and we must make them see beyond that in order to help disabled people. Yes, I know that there are a lot of programs out there to help, but are these programs geared toward really helping all disabled people, or just enough to just keep them stable for the moment? You must really deal with disability up close or have experienced it for yourself to understand the true needs of a disabled person. Once you have that understanding, then when you do begin to advocate, you will know what things to ask for or to put in place for disabled people. In the end, I would like to get the world to understand the support that disabled people need in order to revolt against the inequities in how they are treated, and also teach parents how to be a voice for their disabled children.

Petitioning

Beyond advocating, when we want resources made available, we sometimes must start petitioning. This involves getting a number of people to sign a petition in order to take it to our local governments to begin the conversation about extensive evaluations at treatment centers. At some treatment centers you do not see a psychiatrist you see a psychologist. There is a difference between the two. Although they both do similar task and often work together a psychiatrist goes in depth with their treatment. If a psychologist does not pay close attention to their patient, they can miss something that needs to be addressed by a psychiatrist long term. Without proper evaluations a patient can end up with a wrong diagnosis and just be given medication to help with side effects.

There is also the issue of pain management in treatment centers that needs to be extensively evaluated. Certain medications are given for physical pain as well as mental disorders. Some patients are just given pain medication such as opioids or opiates without further assessment. Some patients are given some of the same medication for mental disorder without seeking further resources. If a patient continues to claim they are in pain or show mental issues the prescription continues without further assessment. This can lead to addiction and overdoses.

Again, we must remember that the government goes by statistics and the medical studies that produce those statistics, and that is how they determine what resources should be made available to the disabled. I do understand that studies and statistics give insight into what is going on with disabled people, but the world also must understand that each disability case is different.

Disabilities are not all on the same level, which means that no one resource will help every disabled person.

One of the biggest things that needs to be petitioned for is the short-term treatment facilities that disabled people go to when they have small episodes. I had the experience of taking my daughter to one, and they only kept her there for a week. She was diagnosed with anxiety and put on medication for that week. Saying that someone who has been acting out just has anxiety is an easy way of pushing treatment under the table. Well, to this day, she still has those outbreaks, and I am still searching for the proper facility to take her to when it happens.

Investing Time

Talking about investing time may seem a little farfetched, especially when you're not gaining anything from it. I would say to think it of it like investing your money. You may get a return financially or you may not. Whether you gain anything or not, wouldn't it be awesome just to see what you have invested into a person who is not able to invest in themselves? For me, I would think so, because I have disabled children, and when I see how far they have come from the time that

I have invested throughout their lives, I am overjoyed and blessed to know that my children are in a better situation today than they were yesterday and every day before that.

Helping others plays a key role in society. We must understand that we are not all the same and that we're all different people, but that does not mean that one is better than the other. For us to help others, we must put in the time and invest in them as we would want someone to do for us. When it comes to disabled people, there are very few who are willing to take the time to help them get where they need to be. I know the task may be difficult, especially when you think of how much you must do and how much time must be invested. Some people want to invest, but physically and mentally they are not able to handle certain situations around them, which is understandable because we're not all built the same when it comes to certain issues. Nevertheless, we must have patience and be willing to go the long haul in order to help disabled people get the resources they need for them to progress and have stable and fruitful lives.

Speaking Out

We must speak out on behalf of disabled individuals, because if we don't, who will? We must understand that their voices are not being heard and they are being pushed into the shadows of society. They walk around like invisible people who aren't even here, and the resources they are getting are minimal because some people think they do not need much to thrive on. So, therefore, we must be their voice. We need to do what it takes to get them the resources that they need to build more stable and fruitful lives. We need to look at what it takes to get them there. We need to write it down, and we need to not just talk about it but be about it. I can say "speak out" all day long, but it must be put into action to get results. Make your voice for them your accountability to do what is right in the world of disabled people.

Creating A Voice

For people with disabilities to have fruitful and stable lives, they must have a voice for themselves. For them to gain and maintain their own voice, they will need the help of the world. They need people to teach them how to see, not just look at the life around them. They need people to hear, not just listen to the conversation around them. They need someone to speak for and with them, not talk about their situation, because all some people do is talk when it comes to helping and getting the proper resources for disabled people. That voice is us, and we need to use it to help them bring their voices up front. I remember growing up, there was always the statement "It takes a village to raise a child." That is very true, and it also takes the world to make sure that the proper resources are put in place for those who are disabled or not able to speak for themselves so that they can have stable and fruitful lives. Most people may feel that it is not their place to worry about people with disabilities and that it is the disabled person's family's job, but God brought us here to love and take care of one another. Therefore, the compassion and love that God has for us and placed in our hearts should be enough to act on.

Conclusion

Imagine being born into a world where you never mattered. Imagine being born into a world where it seemed as though you lived in a square box and were never able to come out. Imagine how it feels to live in containment and being labeled simply because you're disabled, not because you have done anything to anyone. Well, there is a whole society of people who feel that way and have lived that way all their lives.

The fact is, some people act as if they don't care. If they are doing the bare minimum for the disabled, they think that's okay. The bottom line is that disabled individuals will never leave this world. Every day, there are many people who are going to be born disabled or become disabled in some way. We must stand up and not only be a voice for them but help them along with their journey toward having fruitful and stable lives. That journey of helping disabled individuals should also result in these people learning to create a voice for themselves and for others who do not yet have a voice.

www.ingramcontent.com/pod-product-compliance
Lightning Source LLC
Chambersburg PA
CBHW070905280326
41934CB00008B/1591